**ANCHOR
BOOKS**

*THAT FOUR-LETTER
WORD...*

Edited by

Chiara Cervasio

First published in Great Britain in 2003 by
ANCHOR BOOKS
Remus House,
Coltsfoot Drive,
Peterborough, PE2 9JX
Telephone (01733) 898102

HB ISBN 1 84418 195 2
SB ISBN 1 84418 196 0

FOREWORD

Anchor Books is a small press, established in 1992, with the aim of promoting readable poetry to as wide an audience as possible.

We hope to establish an outlet for writers of poetry who may have struggled to see their work in print.

The poems presented here have been selected from many entries, and as always editing proved to be a difficult task.

I trust this selection will delight and please the authors and all those who enjoy reading poetry.

Chiara Cervasio
Editor

CONTENTS

DREAM LOVER

Out of darkened dreams you shone
rhythmic metres metamorphosing
as a child I dreamt of
love's first spiritual ascending

Fleeting clips spent forever
nameless homeless unrevealed
soulful echoing tremors ripple
as angelic songs interfered

Upon elastic wings soaring
bring moments measured
in slumbered moments vampiric times
dawn's breaking song denied us.

Chris Eaton

IN HIS STEAD

A lily knelt o'er his grave,
And whispered a sad refrain:
There is nothing left to save,
Here lies he who strived in vain.

But the wind carried a song.
His love: tombs cannot contain.
Though he dwells where angels throng,
His heart lingers, draped in pain.

Rain drew near with curdling skies,
Falling grace on Earth bewailed:
Should redemption bear no price,
Love's sacrifice would have failed.

As voiced by the lily's hymn,
The heavens drained in his stead
And the breath of life smote him.
Thus, the romance of the dead.

Zardee Emmanuel G Garagan

TOGETHERNESS

Love is an important little word,
Of love there are many different kinds,
There's the love you have for a pet or a child,
My thoughts of love are of two hearts entwined.

We've been together for many years,
We've had our struggles, we've had our strives,
But we've worked together, we've compromised,
But it's our love for each other that's given us a life.

To love someone doesn't always make people happy,
To love someone can also destroy,
A possessive love is unhealthy,
Possessive love should just be for toys.

We've wanted to make each other happy,
That's not always been easy to do,
I think the reason for our happy life together,
Is because neither of us has ruled.

Thank you for your loyalty,
Your gentleness, honesty, your trust,
I can't envisage life without you,
Always by my side, really is a must.

We really are a lucky couple,
I would never wish for anyone else to be by my side,
I never want to lose you,
I want you with me each day till I die.

Gillian S Gill

SHE LOVES

She loves,
And is your friend.
With her,
There is no need to pretend.

She loves,
Every part of you.
With her,
She trusts in what you do.

She loves,
And does not ask why.
With her,
You never have to lie.

She loves,
And will give her all.
With her,
She'll catch you if you fall.

She loves,
Deeply, in every way.
With her,
You're safe, she'll never stray.

Deanna L Dixon

THAT STANDER-BY

He gazed at you from far away.
You knew that he was there.
He saw that you disliked your life
And didn't have a care.
Not one small glance you gave to him,
Not one word would you speak.
His love for you was really strong,
But played like hide and seek.
He also knew that on your own,
Your thoughts were just of pain.
That falling in love with someone else,
Could never be the same.
A man had used your feelings well,
Had tossed your love aside.
You cursed his name, yet loved him still,
Your love just like the tide.
But things just cannot be the same,
And life it must go on.
You've got to take the ups and downs,
As if they were a song.
I suppose you wonder who I am,
Who tells you what to do?
Well I am just that stander-by,
Who truly does love you.

Shadow

My Hopeful Dream

Our dream will last forever,
    always lurking in my heart,
Even though the time has come,
    death's driven us apart.
This gnawing pain of grief I feel
    is very much like fear,
Yet strangely blissful moments come
    as though you're very near.

Perhaps it's just my hope that feels
    you pass by in the wind;
That hears the whisper of your voice
    that touches me again.
Expectant feeling looking up
    to see you at the door,
Alas from dreams I must awake
    for there you are no more.

And yet . . .

Soft measure of your laughter
    seems to blanket me at night.
For just one moment I am saved
    from grasps of grieving fright.
I wait for just these moments
    as I stumble through my day,
Endure this world that you have left;
    so hopelessly I pray
For one more touch of your sweet hand,
    just one more gentle kiss,
One more gaze into your eyes,
    so many things I've wished

And lost within the joy of you;
    so futile now life seems,
Yet you will live forever
    in the hope of my sweet dream.

J A Brown

LOVE'S WHERE, WHEN AND HOW
(A modified sonnet)

O' where are the eyes that squarely met mine?
And where is the touch from your heart?
And where are the arms that for me did entwine
The promise till death do us part!

When did I fail your hopes in me?
When did I never support?
When did I ever turn deaf ears to plea
And, in anger, ever retort?

However can longing now bridge the gap
And how to return to your trust?
How not to let time now drain off the sap
And for love to wither to dust.

In anguish I sit in my room alone:
But if fault is mine, I'll atone.

Ron Hails

FORGET ME NOT

I'll never forget that moment our souls became one,
As our hearts met,
I'll remember all the good times we had,
Laughter and tears,
I'll remember those years,
I'll remember all those angry words,
We shouldn't have said,
That keep going around and around in my head,
I know I'll have to let you go,
So I want you to know,
All the passion and love for you I've got,
Please *forget me not.*

I hope, as time goes by, you will remember me,
As I remember you with love,
I'll never forget and to let you go,
Hurts me so,
And all the passion and love for you I've got I'm asking you,
Please *forget me not.*

I trusted you so much because you said you care,
But then when I needed you the most you just weren't there,
Now the time has come for me to say goodbye,
Take care my love and as I wipe these tears away,
I pray,
All the passion and love for you I've got,
I will *forget you not.*

Angel Hart

Enemy And Lover

I know we have not seen eye to eye
Or been able to speak to each other and smile
Each time we meet we avoid all the while
We know being pleasant would be such a trial

Still I cannot help it if I care about you
Even though I would never declare this true
My heart aches and misses a beat or two
When I hear your name or you enter a room

I have fought these feelings without falling apart
Defended myself by cursing my heart
I've challenged my emotions and relied on the past
To refrain from admitting I'm in love at last

Fifi Smith

WOMEN

The beauty of a woman, I profess
Is not the colour of her dress
But in the mind that she'll process
Her thoughts in

For in this mind, all men must see
They'll find their greatest enemy
For when you have her, her mind is free
And courting

Courting other propositions
In case you falter to a remission
In your all-consuming passion
And stalking

Stalking for that ultimate prize
A glance, a smile, contact of eyes
A show of feeling beyond disguise
Or talking

Talking yet without a sound
She'll pick you up or cut you down
And when the final echoes sound
You're faltering

If you survive her treacherous mind
Are not infatuatedly blind
You may be lucky enough to find
She's caring

Dan Warren

DERYN

Hair like a flaming cresset
Eyes of deepest blue,
Lips so warm and tender
To love, oh how she knew,
Once I was lucky, to both have,
And hold that full but slender frame,
And hear in her ecstatic murmurings
The mention of my name.
Then she went away to college
Coming home each weekend,
Then she said she'd met another
Who was more than just a friend,
Five years we'd been together
My world just fell apart,
She said that she was sorry
But it didn't help my aching heart,
But of all the men who in the past
For her love had made a bid,
Not one, not one single one,
Could have loved her as I did.

E D Bowen

ART

They fall in love themselves one day
With themselves - but that's quite okay
For self-love can be justified,
Every time self-lovers cry

Alone, for self-love causes pain
For all self-love is for self gain
And self gain's the self-lover's art -
It's hard to tell lovers apart.

Peter Asher

DEVASTATED

Listen to the beat of a broken, inflamed, miserable heart
Since you left me for another heart-throb, smiling beau
Seeing you both together sends shivers to every living part
Of my seething, riddled with agony body since the blow
You gave me in the spring of this new year
After months of loving tenderness given by you my love
To a beau that adored and cherished you, my dear
Yet, you suddenly forsook me for a youth, a cove
Who has left you with an unborn child to rear
Alone, in this world, full of heartrending lovers
My heart and soul still love you tenderly my dear
Come back to me, I will be so happy sweetheart
To constantly look after you, your unborn child and clear
Up the mess you have inherited whilst we were apart

Alma Montgomery Frank

WAITING AT THE GATE

When will this be? I can only ask
As I pray that you come my way
If only just for a short while
So we can express our love this way

As into the fields we will go
Together at last for a walk
Holding hands and feeling
No words said, no need to talk

The dogs running in front happily
Unaware of how we feel
To be together for this time
Having these feelings for real

No longer spoken about as dreams
Feelings that can be expressed
With so much love and caring
I truly do feel blessed

When will this be reality?
How much longer do I wait?
Come and show your love for me
I am waiting at the gate.

Christine Cyster

LINGERING IN MEMORY

A smile and a glance, then you asked me to dance,
or was it the other way round?
I only remember a flickering ember,
and suddenly knew I had found,
someone to talk to, to love and to cling to,
a lover as well as a friend,
the ember was glowing, a fire was burning,
a heart that was aching, can mend.

Hands holding tight, in the warmth of the night,
as the music played softly and sweet,
then after a while, you confessed with a smile,
that for dancing, you had two left feet,
I remembered long after, that evening of laughter,
and the wine as it flowed in my veins,
is the best yet to be, or for you and for me,
is a memory all that remains?

You came and you stayed, and we laughed and we played,
and somehow the evening was right,
the loving we shared, was a loving that cared,
yes, it was a beautiful night,
and when you were leaving, I started believing,
that life wasn't really that bad,
the moments of giving, the moments of living,
each day, are the best to be had.

Now the seasons are turning, and still I am learning,
and sometimes I don't understand,
the strings that are pulling us, is God only fooling us,
are we puppets that dance in His hand?
But one thing I know, in the ebb and the flow,
of this life that is given to me,
somewhere in my mind dear, I know I will find dear,
you lingering in memory.

Ellie Tucker

WHEN LOVE DOTH GO UNSEEN

Love doth make the humankind,
Its power is greater than great,
It joins so many people,
In a joyous, happy state.

However, there are times you know,
When love doth go unseen,
And I do feel great anguish,
Because love is so mean.

No matter how much I love her,
She cannot love me back,
For I am a nobody,
To her, a walking tramp.

I smile at her each time I see her,
Sometimes she doth smile back,
But I know she cannot love me
For there are many things I lack.

I lack the simple quality,
Of courage to profess,
To her outstretched bosom,
That I am in distress.

Distress caused by the very love,
The love I have owned for life,
The love for her gentle eyes,
And her conquest over strife.

No matter how much I love her,
She cannot love me back,
For I am an outsider,
And that is sadly that.

Alun Evans

LOVE-IN-A-MIST

Back door was open
I stood for a while
Gazing at the garden
Looked with a smile
At flowers aflutter
Around my toes
But couldn't remember
The right name for those.

What are they called?
Didn't have a clue,
Light, dark and turquoise
All shades of blue.
Opened the books
Scanned down the list -
Ah, now I remember
Love-in-a-mist.

Triggered my mind
Into thinking of us
Cos that's what we had -
All flutter and fuss
The times you were drinking
And wouldn't be kissed,
Those times were our own
Love-in-a-mist.

Sylvia Ross

MY SOULMATE

You mean the world to me,
If only I could make you see,
Make you understand how much I care,
Let you know I'll always be there,
I love you darling, so very much,
Your warmth, your heart, your loving touch,
If I ever lost you, it would be the end,
Of my world and my existence, alone without a friend,
So don't ever leave, stay always by my side,
In times of trouble, always be my guide.

Christine Nolan

FOREVER

I look at the sun to see you there,
smiling eyes and golden hair,
wish that you could be right here
so we can be together

Forever

I look at clouds to see you there,
combing rainbows in your hair,
wish that you could be right here
so we can be together

Forever

I look at the moon to see you there,
laughing eyes and silver hair,
wish that you could be right here
so we can be together

Forever

As you look down to see me here,
chasing daydreams everywhere,
recalling wishes on a star,
we are together

Forever

R N Taber

ALONE AGAIN

Here I am alone again, sitting by myself,
Wondering if I really shall be left upon the shelf.
Here I am alone again, in this empty room,
Wondering if my life will change and if it will, how soon.
Here I am alone again, tired and confused,
Wondering how much longer I'll be stepped upon and used.
Here I am alone again, wondering what love means,
And thinking will I ever meet the person of my dreams.
Here I am alone again, with aching in my heart,
Wondering why it had to end and why we had to part.
Here I am alone again, my eyes so full of tears,
Wondering if the hurt will pass with the coming years.
Here I am alone again, full of hate and pain,
Wondering if I ever shall fall in love again.

S Brown

TRUE LOVE

Flutterings in your stomach,
Blushing when he's around,
Sighing with admiration,
Feeling your heart pound,
Showing that you really care,
Knowing that you've finally found,
The one to share your life forever.

Ann Sykes

HURT TIMES TWO

Hurt times two . . . it was me and you . . . it was she and I
Don't know what happened . . . or why
But now it's you and she . . . don't either of you care . . .
About what happened to me?
One day I was your lover and she was my friend . . .
Next day it was over . . .
And you were with her in the end.
Hurt times two . . . it was me and you . . . it was she and I
I was so happy, she was my friend, and you were my guy
Was it all a lie?
It hurts like Hell! But I'll get by . . .
I'll never forget either one of you . . .
How could you do it to me? I'd never do it to you!
Some say they knew . . . I should have known too
But, it was me and you . . . it was she and I
I couldn't imagine, even if I tried . . .
But when I saw you there . . . *you and her* . . .
It was for sure . . .
Hurt times two . . . and there was nothin' I could do.

Christie Coulter Adams

WHAT IS LOVE, ANYWAY?

What is love, anyway?
As the song so aptly says,
'What's it all about?'
Some days you're floating on air,
Then others down to earth.

Something's said; some unkind word,
And things are never the same.
Sometimes you wish you'd never
Met that red-headed nerd!

Like a little child,
Whose balloon is burst.
The tears start to flow.
What's so bloody marvellous then,
About love; I'd like to know?

Why do we put ourselves through
All that angst and pain?
For a few short months of pleasure?
I don't think I'll bother again!

At least;
That's what I say now,
While the pain and agony's still raw.
But then, love's like a lottery.
It's all in the luck of the draw!

Perhaps tomorrow I'll meet
Prince Charming - who'll
Sweep me off my feet.
He'll whisper sweet nothings
And I'll find myself drowning again,
In a sea of impossible dreams,
That are destined to go down the drain!

Susan Forest

SEPARATE ROADS

I'm on the move again, it's time to make a new start,
motoring back south, trying to remedy a broken heart.
The car's packed, it's time for those painful goodbyes,
goodbye Lancashire, where the truth, where the lies.

Last minute surprise, I didn't think I'd see you again,
travelling together, London-bound in the heavy rain.
The road's been long, at Towcester we stop to dine,
oak-panelled restaurant, wishing you could be mine.

It's just like a fairy tale romance, this weekend alone,
but like all such tales, the magic can only be on loan.
Reaching the East End, and just one possible conclusion,
two separate roads, for this love can only be an illusion.

Keith Leese

TIME

We met and time was ours to share,
We laughed and loved, had time to care.
A love which lasted through the years,
Times of joy and times of tears.
Then came the time of quiet days
To love you and your gentle ways.
We did not know the time was near
When we must part - the sudden fear
Of life too short - dark nights a haze
Clinging to our final days.
Our last goodbye - a memory
Which time will never dull for me.

Merle Sadler

GONE

If love be life, then life from me was stole.
My memory to me is only death.
Where once was life there is now but a hole,
Which draws from me tormented final breath.
And in this state of death, in which I live,
I wander ghost-like searching for a way
To lose this shroud I wear, and I would give
My soul to live for just another day.
My life and hers were bound with bands of steel
A lifetime in two years, we spent as one,
We shared the sorrow, laughter and the tears
There was no thing we could not overcome;
'Til jealousy on us his finger lay
In sorrow leaving me to lonely stray.

Alex L Jones

PROMISE ME

Promise me that you will not
give your heart to another lover,
and that you'll still remember me
when the blossom's on the tree.

Promise me that you'll wait for me
if we should ever part,
that you'll always keep a place for me
so close to your heart.

Promise me that you won't give
your sweet kiss to any other lover,
as I don't want to share your love
with another.

Promise me that you will not give
your heart to another lover,
as it would only break my heart
as I can love no other.

K Lake

WHISPERS

I could hear your voice calling
in the early evening breeze
as the warmth of the night
filled the swaying trees
I remember when we walked
along those country lanes
holding hands, laughing
we had love in our veins
all those precious moments
keep on jogging my memory
your face so very clear
just like my vanity
if only I had listened
to the wake up call
should have sensed the drifting
read the writing on the wall
then in the silence of the night
again I hear your voice
it seemed to say you let me go
but you did not have a choice.

David Tye

I THOUGHT

The rain was flooding the streets,
I took a picture of you in the wind.
You looked away and smiled,
our sun was still shining inside.

I came back home a month ago
to find you packing your stuff ready to go.
I tried to ask why,
you just turned away and said goodbye.

I found your message on the phone,
you sounded sorry and couldn't understand what for.
See, I've heard all such stories before,
plus, I still haven't cleared your broken picture off the floor.

I thought I heard you crying across the walls the other night,
I thought I heard you whispering my name,
but I'm afraid the wind was playing tricks again.

I thought I heard the radio playing the other day,
I thought I heard you singing away.
I thought I felt your lips on mine as I switched off the light,
I'm sure you felt my arms embracing you all night.
But I'm afraid both our hearts were being fooled again.

Giovanni Nacci

I MISS YOU

A little bit of you,
A little bit of me,
Have switched respective places,
In a mystifying we.

When miles come between us,
And our lives are drawn apart,
Our thoughts remain together,
Tugging softly at the heart.

This loneliness without you,
Tells of special moments shared,
And says across the miles,
Just how much you have cared.

The emptiness that comes,
With just the memory of your touch,
Stirs a feeling from within that says,
I miss you very much.

Shauneen Malone

IRRESPONSIBLE LOVE

I've fallen in love so many times,
When the world was young and gay.
Yet somehow, it wasn't a disaster
When my loved one went away!

My youth was spent in wartime,
If *he* wasn't posted, it was *me!*
We lived with death and forgetting.
'Give up on the things that can't be!'

Lasting love is forged by association.
Not brief, breathless intimacy,
But the romance of life is the memory
Of when one loved so recklessly!

Joyce M Jones

CUPID'S ARROW

Like a shaft of golden light,
Love will touch your heart,
Sometimes, just to stay awhile,
Or - never to depart.

Oh! So many forms of love,
But one alone is special.
It seems to only come the once,
Ignore it - at your peril!

Exciting, overwhelming, powerful,
A feeling, like no other,
You are in his arms - forsaking all else,
Pledging love, for one another.

Some search a lifetime for a love,
Or settle for lesser, a brew!
Lucky indeed are they who find,
A soulmate with love ever true.

Love is a joy, a comfort, a pain,
Your emotions are in such a whirl!
The world becomes a wonderful place,
For an 'arrow-struck' boy and girl!

E M Eagle

TODAY

The flowers I would have taken,
The kind words I would have said,
If I had known her earthly life
Was so near to its end.

But I put off till tomorrow
What I should have done that day,
And my heart is filled with vain regrets,
And sadness and dismay.

These words I pen in sorrow,
These words I pen today,
Do not wait until tomorrow
Do the good now, while you may.

For tomorrow's in God's keeping,
'Tis today that you must heed,
If you'd help someone in sickness,
If you'd aid someone in need.

For all the heartfelt sorrow,
And all the tears are vain,
When the object of your good intent
Has shed this mortal frame.

G E Chambers

THERE IS NO ESCAPE

The pain, the pain, the awful pain
The creeping stealth o'er fibre and vein
The short sharp breaths, the aching heart
The tearing and ripping of dreams apart
It starts in the stomach and rises like fire
It sticks in the throat, like a moth in a mire
There is no escape, sleep steals away
Like a dye in clear water, the pain's here to stay
What went wrong? What shattered the dream?
What ripped our love from seam to seam?
We started off so strong together
I gave you trust forever and ever
I placed my faith in your strong hands
I never dreamed you would break the bands
That bound us strong as one pure soul
We'd love forever, a common goal
How could you leave me, how could you be so cruel?
You explore new pastures since dumping this fool
For fool I am and fool I'll stay
I cannot move on since that fateful day
I go through the motions for all to see
I smile at them when they smile at me
But inside this body, like a searing flame
A twisting knife, mutilation and maim
There is no escape from this awful pain
I see your face at the close of night
And taste your taste with the dawning light
There is no escape, for with every breath
I'll breathe your name till the day of my death
There is no escape!

B Hawkins

A MORTAL BLOW

I'm sorry I'm not the guy
To share my life with you
For I'm still very confident
That's all I want to do

When you said you loved me
I planned my life ahead
Now you've changed your mind my dear
That life I simply dread

I'm sorry I'm not the guy
To lead you down the aisle
To wipe away your every tear
And enjoy your every smile

I'm sorry that all my hopes and all my dreams
Beneath the heavens above
Are never going to be shared
With the one I love

The thought of little children
Belonging to you and myself
Can not compare with anything
Not even wealth

I'm sorry I'm not the guy
To watch your hair turn grey
For believe it or not but this heart which I've got
I know will love you always

Desiree L P Silsby

AGAINST THE ODDS
(Dedicated to my husband . . . 'Ain't nobody')

Without him I am nothing
With him I am whole
They said our love would never last
The passion would burn cold

Without him I am lost at sea
With him I am found
They said too many hearts would break
There was no common ground

Without him there's no meaning
With him I'm complete
They said that only fools rush in
Where angels would retreat

Without him there's no reason
With him there's a point
They said that in the darkness
We'd never find the light

With him there is sunshine
Without him only rain
They said after the rainbow
There would be only pain

Against the odds we never listened
It fell upon deaf ears
So glad I never went away
So glad that you're still here

Jo-Ann Waldron-Hall

SHEDDING SKIN

You don't look to see my face,
crumbling in the rain.
Don't know that I breathe you
again and again.

Though I'll soar Red Admiral,
you've drained me of colour,
caging a moth that will
cry like no other.

You don't care for fragile wings,
hovering on your fence.
It inconveniences you to think
about the skin of something else.

Is this what you always planned,
So stark black and white?
Can't you search for something deeper
than *the girl is not right*?

I can't re-spin the silken film
that blushed upon my skin.
Can't change the dates that history bled
to leave you out of them.

You won't look to see my face
crumbling in the rain.
Won't know that I turn back
again and again . . .

Catriona Yule

MY LOVE IS LIKE A SWEET WILD ROSE
(With apologies to Robert Burns)

My love is like a sweet wild rose,
So delicate and fair,
My love is like the windswept corn,
With golden waving hair.

And for the nectar I will long,
That's only giv'n by thee,
And, as the lark repeats his song,
I'll ever constant be.

And I will woo thee, bonnie lass,
Until thy heart is won,
And I will love thee still, my lass,
As long as shines the sun.

As long as shines the sun, my lass,
As long as rivers run,
And I will love thee still, my lass,
As long as shines the sun.

Muriel Willa

IS IT LOVE?

Is it love that shines within your eyes
When you gaze back at me
Or am I only dreaming?
Seeing what I yearn to see?

Do you often think about me
When I can't be with you?
Wish that I were in your arms
Or are thoughts of me so few?

Do I take your breath away
When I enter a room?
Does your heart beat wildly
Beneath a full romantic moon?

And does it lift your spirits
To hear a softness in my voice?
And fill your world with gladness
Knowing I'm with you through choice?

If you do feel all these things
And I suspect you do.
Then I can tell you with open heart
You are my dream come true.

W A Ronayne

THE LOVE I LOST

We met and loved each other dearly
But he had to go away
I had no message or letter
While he was ordered to stray

I did not know if he really cared
And I could not find it out
So I eventually married
But afterward I had my doubt

It did not last, as I should have known
But we had a little girl
My mum and dad helped me in all this
They never knew and I did not unfurl

My husband and I came together
And had a few years of life
But he died young and left me alone
And then I had years of strife

Many times I thought of my lost love
Many regrets have I known
But it is all too late now to replace
The love I lost has ever grown

I shall not forget that love I knew
And to me it will remain
I'll never know if it would have worked
But it will always bring pain

Edith Buckeridge

DESTINY

This one; who cradles every dream
Unleashes all with constant beam
Descended star, within my reach
His glowing core, my soul to teach
And with each glance, I'm held in awe
This man, for whom, the search was for

For fate offered our paths to cross
But if no path, my worldly loss
Yet fear I do, my soul will burst
He is my juice, to quench my thirst
'You are my life!' my vital air
The one, the gift; the answered prayer

Kerry Feild

TO MY GRIEF!

To my grief I fell for you
Towards a bottomless hell
And withered was my coloured flower
And sour was the smell
Time that passed so quickly and fast
Brought weight upon my feet
And when I fell towards my hell
My heart became concrete
Spoke just two words to take my smile
Another four took my tears
Five minutes to my great surprise
Lasted many years
So it is safe to say my friend
That great love leads to sorrow
But if from fear we never love
We will never know what follows

Paul McAnearney

I'LL GET OVER YOU

I was oblivious, I never knew
The pain you were going through
You never talked to me
You never even said goodbye
I found out I was history
When I went home and found it empty

I'll get over you
I'll find someone new
I've been down before
I'll keep coming back for more

I did love you with all my heart
It's sad when you have to part
It means making a new start
When I'm in my bed
I can't get you out my head
I think about the words I left unsaid

Now at the end of the day
Those words I didn't say
Would they have made a difference anyway
You have made it quite clear
You don't want to be here
Quite frankly I don't give a damn dear

I'll get over you
I'll find someone new
I've been down before
I'll keep coming back for more

Michael McNulty

PLEASE GOD, HEAL MY PAIN

Why did you hurt me so?
The depth of pain you'll never know!
I loved you so much,
I still miss your touch.
A love you might never know again.
Only time can heal my pain.
My head throbs because of a broken heart.
Why was it us who had to part?
My emotions run deep,
But a flicker for you I'll always keep,
In time my anger will fade away
And one bright sunny day
I'll realise too,
There is life after you!

Brenda E Cheeseman

FIRST LOVE

My first love was a boy at school,
I could never forget his name.
Andrew ignored me to my shame,
I remember he thought me a fool.
It's true I was the dunce of the class,
The one I felt everyone laughed at.
It wasn't my fault I was ugly and fat,
Daydreaming to make the time pass.

We grew up and went our separate ways,
I lost weight and became nice and slim.
Would we meet again one of these days?
A few years later I worked in a gym.
He didn't recognise me as I met his gaze,
I was the personal trainer assigned to him.
It certainly seemed a strange place to meet,
And I can honestly say that revenge is sweet!

Rosemary Davies

MY TEARS ON YOUR SHOULDER

My tears on your shoulder
Will soon be dry and no more
And as you walk through your bedroom door
Will you think of me as she touches you
As I caressed you a few hours before?
My time with you is my treasure
Your mind, your body - my pleasure.
Come lay with me tomorrow
When I promise to hide my sorrow
And my tears on your shoulder
Will soon be dry and no more.

Sara Bella

MY HEART

Why does the love we share have so much pain for us to feel?
Are we blinded by our emotions, is what we feel totally real?
The pain, the love, the heartache and all the hurt,
One minute you're in Heaven, the next as low as dirt,
Love has always been like this from our very first heartbeat,
Love hurts everyone, from the big and strong to the small and weak,
Love and hurt walk hand in hand, they go together like hand and glove,
One minute you're at each other's throats and the next thing
                                        totally in love,
Don't ever underestimate love or you'll feel the pain that comes
                                        with it too,
If you've ever fallen in love before, then you know what I say is true,
Everyone's love is different, but our hearts all feel the same
                                        joy and pain,
Being torn between the love and the heartache, can drive
                                        your mind insane,
Love will never ever change, you'll feel in Heaven and you'll
                                        feel so fine,
But before you go and fall in love, remember what comes
                                        with it in time.

Karl A Hunter

MORNING

Familiar contempt
    between the pair
as silence dances
    in the air
realisation
    at love's joke
there's no fire
    without the smoke
long quelled by kids
    and needful things
no love left
    in the rings

R M Membury

ENTWINED IN INTIMACY

whispered words
lovers heard
to inspire implore
empathise adore

lingered look
thrill to tenterhook
emote enlighten
feelings heighten

tingling touch
on fingers clutch
as caress cleave
delights perceive

lips so tactile
sensuous smile
faculty febrile
conjoin while

twinned thoughts
embrace cherish
clasp surrounds
desire abounds

passion pulsate
consummate sublimate
entwined intimate
together as one

Brian Strand

FROM HIM TO HER

I love the way you look tonight
Your eyes are such a wonderful sight,
You are the one I love,
Your face is as white as a dove.

You look so lovely in a dress of lace,
And the pale white of your face,
I miss you so much when you go away,
But you have come back to me today.

Your lips are red like a rose,
And with your perfect nose,
Your hair is charcoal black,
You are the one I lack.

Your teeth are so white,
They shine like a light,
Your eyes are so blue,
I love you and I need you.

C Murray

SORRY TO SAY

Sorry if I am being unreasonable
In the things I say and do,
But you have to give me time
I have a lot of stuff to get through.

Sorry if you are offended
With the way that I am feeling,
But put yourself in my shoes
You too, I think, would be reeling.

Sorry if you think I am dragging out
All that has happened in the near past,
But I've tried so hard to dismiss
What has happened and heal my heart.

Sorry but from you I need total commitment
Feel loved and know you want me here,
You trying to understand my emotions
My betrayal and my fear.

Sorry if this is all too much to ask
But the trust will not return straight away,
It will take time and patience
That is all at this minute I can say.

Sorry but try to put yourself where I was
Would you have handled it better than me?
Because I do not think that you would
The cost to you would have been too dear.

Sorry if you think I should now move on
How I wish that it could so be
But I would not be in this position
If you had not hurt and humiliated me.

Time, they say, is a great healer
Bad memories will fade into the past
Be able to look to the future
With optimism our being together, will last.

Margaret M Donnelly

OUR LOVE

A love like ours should never die,
Now I will give you the reasons why.
Two people who are truly in love,
Say their marriage is made in Heaven above.
You will have your fights and have your mirth,
It's trying to find your partner's worth.
The making-up is the best part,
Loving each other from the heart.
You may break a home up in your fight,
Whatever you do, do not take flight.
Stay and listen, then talk it through,
But do not walk out whatever you do.
Remember that you love each other,
And save yourself a lot of bother.

Zoe French

Waiting In The Wings

Like a leading lady who steals the stage,
Yet with indifferent eye applies her art,
With a bland strolling player you engage,
Who borrows my lines and mimics my part.
Offstage I stand in the wings and rehearse,
To rouse my tongue to sing all your praises,
To make you subject to my winning verse,
To express my love with precious phrases.
Then, with a gesture, you give me my cue,
But tongue-tied by fear, my boldness subsides.
I forfeit my hour on the stage with you,
And my overtures falter into asides.
Your leading man's role was my chief desire,
But I swapped my suit for a clown's attire.

John Dickie

OFF THE BALL

He suffered for love, but still he would try.
A broken arm and a big black eye.

3 days in a prison cell.
A visiting ban that hurt like hell.

A family who rejected him.
Thrown in a strange river, when he could not swim.

Thrown off his Mecca, the field of green.
The whole angry atmosphere made him mean.

Still a loyal follower, a passionate man.
These are the sacrifices of a football fan.

Trevor Napper

CHANCE MEETING

They both met at an auction bidding for the same old chair,
He to match the other one at home to make the pair,
She, to add some furniture to the flat that she had bought,
He outbid her by a mile for the thing she sought,
Homeward bound she thought of him, a tall, nice-looking chap,
He could not remember her, as he headed for his flat,
They next met at the bedding sale, both searching for a bed,
She spotted what she wanted, and just beat him by a head.

The supermarket, their next call, among the aisles they met,
He still could not remember her, she could not forget,
He helped her lift her shopping up, to load it in the boot,
She thanked him with her cutest smile, this time he had a look,
And thought of her all the way home, as she did think of him,
Now they recall each other, and not just with a whim,
For she made an impression, as he had done with her,
And both hoped they would meet again, some other time, somewhere.

Another auction loomed for them, again they did attend,
He to find a writing desk, her an antique pen,
To match the set she had at home, a gift from years gone by,
Maybe she'd find one at the same, maybe she'd catch his eye,
He noticed her across the room, and watched her make her bid,
She noticed him watching her, and lost the pen she did,
She watched him buy the writing desk, and smiled when he lost out,
To the person at the auction who made the sudden shout.

And outbid him to get the desk, the one he wanted so,
She wanted the antique pen, but had to let it go,
After the sale they finally spoke, she offered him the desk,
Which he accepted only if, she took from him the pen,
They visit the sales together now, to furnish their new home,
Both knowing each one's wishes, for now they bid as one,
And as with all love stories, a happy ending does prevail,
All through a mere chance meeting, at an antique auction sale.

K Townsley

NEVER, NEVER AGAIN

I have loved three men, never again,
Charming, blue-eyed, fair-haired men, never again.
Did they love me? I cannot tell,
Their loving turned my life to hell,
I loved them more than words reveal, never again.

The first in my youth, never again,
I believed in his truth, never again.
Innocence was my only guide,
He was beautiful, married, lied,
I loved him 'til the day he died, never again.

The second rescued me, never again,
His love was clear to see, never again.
Married while still broken-hearted,
Love blossomed, quickly departed,
Died before life ever started, never again.

The third was my heaven, never again,
My heart so riven, never again.
Obsession gripped my heart and soul,
I worshipped and adored too well,
He took my all, left me alone, never again.

The moral of this? Never again,
That love is a gift, never again.
Happiness is very fleeting,
Giving as well as receiving,
But guard your heart in your own keeping, *never again.*

Caroline Isherwood

SO HUMBLE

I've tried through all as best I can,
To be so right, your loving man,
The rest of care and all to share,
In love alone, one can compare,
A life may settle in abyss,
With thoughts and tears, a loving kiss,
To gather in, a hope proclaim,
You're loving touch, oft call your name,
Each sigh contained a thought so dear,
So humble see, beyond my sphere,
How can this be real? I feel aware,
Each gentle touch, we'd e'er but share,
I know you love me too my dear,
Of one so precious, I feel a tear,
A happiness my heart to sing,
Your lips met mine, of joyous cling,
Someone to share with all my life,
I'm here for you dear, please be my wife,
A husband to be, we'll share our lives,
Through all come may, have each survives,
When future casts its weary name,
We'll find through all bothers we still feel the same,
And if family comes too, we will have such bliss,
Of Heaven created, to be like this,
A son to consider, two daughters as true,
Each loving care in the shape of them, you.

Hugh Campbell

As I Mean To Go On

I can't help being the way I am,
Feeling the things I feel.
My fears like my love for you,
Are so very real.
I try saying to myself,
Our love will never end,
But then I know I can't be so certain,
And the fears start over again.
I try not to take you for granted,
Or smother you too much,
I just want you to feel wanted,
And know that you are loved.
Is it so wrong that I love you
So much so that I would die of a broken heart
If we were to ever hurt each other so much
That our love would just fall apart?
Is it such a terrible thing
That I want you for my own,
And if our love was to ever die,
I would rather spend the rest of my life alone?
I don't care about the money I spend
Or the sacrifices that I make.
For you I would do anything,
Whatever it would take,
To keep you loving me forever,
And sharing in this life.
The joys of spring,
The cold of winter.
Holding hands in the daytime,
Cuddling up at night.
Just the two of us at first,
Then maybe some childer of our own,
A dingy little apartment in the beginning,
Then our own real home.

Then I would like for us to grow old together,
Telling the grandchildren stories of our youth.
Before we die in each other's arms,
And instead of saying goodbye,
We will whisper, 'I love you'.

David Tiplady

I Don't Want To Know

I don't want to know.
Your reasoning isn't fair.
Love with you is not a thing to share,
Yet I can't bear to let you go,
And so I break down.
When you are around,
I let my feelings show.
It's just a state of mind.
My emotions leave me blind.
The turmoil of the hurt goes on inside.
Your infidelity came as a bitter blow,
So now in stunned silence I walk alone,
Living in this house, no longer my home.
You don't even care to phone.
So here, my tears become a tide
From a spring welling up inside,
Flowing deep into another lonely night.
Please give me back your love.
I'm only made of flesh and blood.
My heart's not a soulless piece of wood.
Come home and switch on your loving light.
Let me again see all the things rainbow-bright.

Jonathan Pegg

FARAWAY DAYS

Faraway days will always come,
Shining, mystical, the haunting sun.
Faraway days will always come,
It can never be undone.

Your name is my meaning.
You became the dreaming.
The skies were gleaming light.
My tears were streaming bright.
Those faraway days I'd fight.
Those faraway days I'd write:

You are my everything.
You are the birds that sing.
You are the stars and moon.
You are the lilting tune.

Faraway days did start,
Ringing the bells of my heart.
Walking slowly mile after mile,
Then that day you gave me your smile:

You are my everything.
You are the birds that sing.
You are the stars and moon.
You are the lilting tune.

Faraway days will always come,
Shining, mystical, the haunting sun.
Faraway days will always come,
It can never be undone.

Faraway days are yours and mine.
Faraway days always take time.
Faraway days will always come,
Shining, mystical, the haunting sun.

Carol Ann Darling

Bitter Words Spoken

Bitter words spoken, love finally coming to an end.
Lost the love of my life, lost my one and only friend.
Words that would ease my pain don't come easily.
Life in a dream, what is finally left for me.

My lover's moon above has finally lost its glow.
Lost the love, lost the heart, this man used to know.
Life of love gone now, no more to have again.
Life of the dreamer, for me to live in pain.

Warm were the nights as we lay side by side.
Love in a broken heart, today has finally died.
A life of loneliness, lost dreams just a memory.
A life of emptiness is all that's left for me.

No sun, so warm appears in my grey skies.
Bitter words remembered, untruths, the lies.
Boxes filled with two lives, ready, waiting to go.
Years of loving now forgotten, two people on show.

Losing loved ones, friends, this happens to all.
New friendships begin, growing strong, trees grow tall.
Life carries on, in time things begin to mend.
We find new lovers, best of all, a new friend.

Kevin Collins

LOVE

Love is humble, love is kind,
Locked in our hearts, deep in our minds,
Our hearts feel love no matter what the age,
We still feel love, but do not hate,
Some never find their perfect mate,
The words we say, from deep within our hearts,
Keep us together, and not apart.

For life without must be so empty,
A time to share a life of plenty,
To share the good times with the bad,
A better life with love will be had,
To look back over life's ups and downs,
Sometimes a smile, sometimes a frown.

But through it all, if we work together,
Share the sun and the stormy weather,
Life can be good, it's there to take,
Happiness in life is what you make it,
So share the smiles, wipe away the tears,
And make your love last for years and years.

Wendy Walker

REALM OF ANGELS

If you ever see an aura
Or hazy flickering light
It is your guardian angel
Making sure that you're alright

You may even feel
The fluttering of wings
Softly, gently guiding you
To the right path life brings

The angelic realm has many
Mysterious ways and forms
Especially when things go wrong
Through strife, pain and storms

Remember they are waiting
In them to confide
Never far away
Watching by your side

Abundance of skilful angels
This you'll surely find
For different situations
All carefully assigned

Next time that you feel
An angel close at hand
Open up your mind to them
Find what they have planned

Angels bring you joy and hope
And bright showers of love
These radiant guardian angels
Sent to you from above

Patricia Carter

WE PAY ALL THE WHILE
(Dedicated to Faye)

As I lay my head on my pillow
Suddenly - the tears begin to flow

Without you by my side
The pain I try to hide

I miss kissing you goodnight
Instead - I cuddle your pillow tonight

It's all those loving feelings I still keep
Above all our friendship so meaningful and deep

As I recall all those future plans we made
Pictures of our past run through my head

When I close my eyes - I can see your face
Remembering the warmth of each other's embrace

The memories through my mind I chase
Spiritual moments I would not erase

I still feel - you know all the while
Hidden beneath your tormented smile

Even though you've left an empty space
Your pillows kept warm by my face

Graham Hare

COMPLETE BLISS

My skin burns where you touch it, with fingers light as air.
My heart and mind contain your smile, your gaze so full of care.
I'm breathing in the scent of you and feel your heart beat fast,
This moment is so precious, I pray for it to last.
Your voice is so impossibly low, it soothes like a caress,
Your hands so clever and adept have caused my swift undress.
A line from your nose to your sensitive mouth, a record of
                                                your laughter,
Problems fade, when we're as one, we'll live happily ever after.

Sophie Jordanov

VALENTINE

Wherever you are and whatever you do
My arms are outstretched, waiting for you
I love you continuous, by day and by night
Love is tremendous, like a comet in flight.

Like a river meandering, drifting along
Love songs we favour, all going strong
Sun and the moon, all planets above
Stars that are countless, so is my love.

One thing is certain, love never grows old
Seasons keep changing, love remains bold
Love that is tender makes us tender too
So never ending continues life through.

No one can say, when we'll meet again
But love changes not, while still I remain
Our destiny is for us both not to be together
Not just a lifetime, but ever and ever.

I said when I met you sweet valentine
This love will endure all test of time
That very first moment I had you in sight
When comes the darkness, you are my light.

Joan Prentice

SOON

Soon I will be seeing you again,
My heart will leap, as always, this I know,
Of all of them, you are the best of men.

No matter who I meet, or where I go,
My mind and memory travel back to you.
Perhaps because I long to hold you so.

There's part of you in everything I do,
You're there when I'm awake or when I dream,
I cannot wait our friendship to renew.

You listen when I want to let off steam,
And never judge, no matter what I say.
You're my source of inspiration, my main theme.

I hate each moment while you are away.
Soon you will be here, but not today.

Joyce Walker

To My Valentine

I'm sending you this greeting
On Valentine's day
And hope that all these wishes
Will always come your way.

To have peace in your heart
From day to day
And love that is shared
Along the way.

To wake each day
In the morning sun
In a world without fear
When the day is done.

To love one another
As I know I love you
This is my Valentine
Especially for you.

Alice Rowe

THE WONDER OF LOVE

Love is a many splendoured thing,
It sings a song in your heart and what joys it does bring.
When you find you're in love for the very first time, when love
                                    comes knocking upon your door,
The feeling is lovely, warm and divine and will stay with you
                                    for evermore,
Because of this new lovely feeling you've found,
You feel all light-headed, you're floating amongst the stars,
Mingling with the great ones, such as Jupiter and Mars,
It is a wonderful feeling to be deeply in love,
To become one together like two turtle doves,
The feeling of love for someone will be with you tomorrow,
                                    today and for evermore.
Because to love one another is what we're put on this earth for,
For love never leaves you, it stays within your heart,
It is a very special part of us, it's within us from the start,
Love is a feeling, when you're overcome with joy,
It's like when you hear the cry of a newborn baby girl or boy,
Love is a thing that grows, it gets bigger each and every day,
The love we give should be pure and come deep within our heart,
It should always be with us and never apart,
Love is being honest and loving, giving and it's the thing that makes
                                    all our lives worth living,
Love is a fragile and a very special thing and it's something
                                    we all should share,
It makes a difference in our lives knowing someone cares,
When you have special people in your lives, that you love
                                    with all your heart,
You love them forever and their presence you will treasure,
Love is giving all your affection and devotion, sticking together,
Through life's ups and downs, going through the motions,
And after all this, if you survive life's stormy waters,
You will hear those magic words that will come shining through,
Because all those people will say I love you,

And then you will truly know that to be loved in your life then
                                        you are truly blessed,
Because the only things important in life are your health,
                                        love and happiness.

Toni Attew

YOUNG STUDENT DAYDREAM

As I sit here at my study
I raise my eyes awhile,
To see in nearby window
A baby's beaming smile.

A joy to those who love him,
No doubt beyond compare,
He sets my mind a-wandering
As I see him playing there.

I think of all the happy times
That we have yet to come,
Knowing now that you are mine,
And that we two are one.

As my thoughts return to study,
And my eyes to books return,
They fall upon your photo -
And I hasten on to learn.

Douglas Bryan Kennett

ALL YOU NEED TO DO

I just love seeing you walk.
I just love hearing you talk.
I just love feeling your touch.
I just love wanting you so much.
    Just being you,
That's all you need to do.

I just love watching your eyes.
I just love listening to your sighs.
I just love you, come rain or shine.
I just love knowing you're mine.
    Just being you,
That's all you need to do.

I just love to hold you tight.
I just love kissing you goodnight.
I just love sharing your fun.
I just love that I'm the one.
    Just being you,
That's all you need to do.

Dave Sim

HEART SAKE

There's a maggot in my heart
It's bored its way inside
Tearing out the soul of me
And eating at my pride
It was put there by a beauty
A dancing butterfly
That's locked itself inside my heart
Until the day I die
Unless you say 'I love you'
And dispel this gnawing doubt
It will carry on inside of me
Slowly eating its way out
Leaving just a hollow shell
Where once my love was stored
Leaving me in earthly hell
Not loving any more

Harry Lyons

MY LOVE

My love for you is a hunger
From deep down inside
Within my heart
Where my soul hides

All my senses
Send messages there
Making it pound
For you are around

It only aches
When we are apart
For then it's an organ
No longer a heart.

Margaret Pow

QUEEN OF STARLESS NIGHT

When no stars shine, will you be mine?
When first I saw your face divine
You seared my soul, refreshed like wine
The refined product of fine vines

So Tracey if one day we kiss
Then would I taste the route to bliss
The rapture, tenderness I miss
You could start Tracey with one kiss

Well I know Tracey I'll be poor
Unless my soul with yours will sour
For you're the one that I adore
This gentle fever has no cure

But Tracey don't believe the fiction
That love I feel is an addiction
For you explode like dynamite
The queen of every starless night.

Phil McLynn

SHOULD I

Should I love you?
Would you make me happy
Or would I end up blue?

Should I take a chance,
Give you my heart,
Give into love and romance?

I would love you forever
And be true till the end
But if should you hurt me
My heart would never mend

If you should ever leave me
I would surely die
Can I give you my love?
I ask myself why

I look into your eyes
Please tell me
Should I?

Maurice McAlister

HOW MUCH?

I love you as high as the moon and the stars,
As deep as the ocean so blue,
I love you as wide as the world and back,
As far as it takes to reach you.

I love you as warm as a hot summer's day,
As bright as the sun in the sky,
I love you as big as a mountain range,
And I will till the day that I die.

I love you as sweet as the birdsong at dawn,
So cheerful, clear and true,
I love you as long as the winding road,
So long as it leads back to you.

I love you as strong as a hurricane storm,
As calm as a mill pond, so still,
I love you with every breath that I take,
With each beat of my heart, I always will.

K E Evans

MY VALENTINE

Hearts and flowers,
Halcyon hours,
Years gone by,
And how they fly.
Memories cling,
Thus to bring,
Thoughts to mind,
When I was yours and you were mine
Each the other's Valentine.

Joy of living,
Both loving, giving,
Felt so much,
With lips that touched,
Now it seems,
They were just dreams,
Our love sublime,
Not dimmed by time,
I still am yours and you are mine,
Each the other's Valentine.

Ellen Thompson

I'D DO ANYTHING FOR YOU

(For 'Magot')

I'd crawl on glass and rusty nails,
I'd brave the sun and winter gales.
I'd pick on men, and them I'd fight,
I'd place my hand in fire bright.

I'd drive a nail through my left hand,
On burning coals I'd freely stand.
On motorbike I'd jump a bus,
And when I'm ill I wouldn't fuss.

My plate collection I'd throw away,
I'd wash and wipe the pots each day.
I'd take the dogs a walk each night,
When you're wrong I'd say you're right.

I'd steal a car, then give it back,
My will to please would never slack.
I'd climb a cliff and then jump off,
I'd pretend I'm ill and fake a cough.

I'd stand in rain till I'm wet through,
These things you know I'd do for you.
There's not a thing that I won't do,
And all because you love me true.

Garry Knowles

YOU'RE MARRIED TO HIM, BUT . . .

I love the smile on your face,
The sparkle in your eye.
The way your nose twitches
When you tell him a lie.

I love the scent of your perfume,
The taste on your lips.
The dark secret in your eyes,
Hiding a total eclipse.

I love the sound of your voice
When it races, when it stalls,
I love you when you're speechless,
Just a look that says it all.

I love the way your body moves,
The sensuality in your dance.
The way your erogenous zones
Send messages of romance.

I love the way you melt
Into my warm embrace.
I love you whispering promises,
I'm a winner in a one horse race.

I love everything about you,
From your head down to your toes.
Why he doesn't see you
Through my eyes, God only knows.

It's so easy to love you,
Even though you're not mine.
You may be married to him
But you're my Valentine.

Terry Traynor

CANDLE

With a lick of flame
The candle wicks I light
Oh, your heart I want to tame
The candles reveal your eyes so bright
A gust of wind the room blows in
The slight chill draws us near
The candles flicker, the room goes dim
I steal a kiss, and fear
For your love is elsewhere, and it's not right
But love is strong, for it's my heart taken
The candle burns out, and brings in the night
I've taken that chance and feel shaken
It's love at its strongest
And it's melting my heart
This night, the longest
I've known from the start

N L Coles

LOST MOMENT!

'Twas just by chance
a meeting of paths,
momentarily crossed.
Both out for a dander
individually,
pleasant meander.

Spontaneous distraction
heated passion,
intense reaction.
No words said
or need be spoken,
transfixingly faltered
spellbound,
held unbroken.

But cut to the quick
it's lost - slick,
unable to stick.
Magical moment
shot - unspent.
Time moves on
fate strayed,
emotions betrayed.

Gary J Finlay

A Special Day (Sonnet)

The flowers will be delivered by ten,
Those wrapped bouquets that they always neaten -
Enclosed are words from my favourite pen,
And with love's fine wine, the day will sweeten.
From this day on will our true love alter?
This day, will you ever leave me lonely?
Will love's nimble feet dance and not falter,
Vowing to remain my one and only?
Each year the tide of love does not relent -
Written from the heart, my words are innate.
This day of love is a magic event,
I'm looking forward to our dinner date.
Doubts will softly and suddenly vanish,
I heard you pray - last night I heard your wish.

Olliver Charles

REMEMBER TO 14TH!

On this date, one month ago,
A great thing happened,
That we know!
To a certain jeweller
You and I sped;
That was the day
We engaged to be wed!

It seems so strange,
That a month has passed;
But we'll arrange
To make our love last;
Elusive it was,
But lasting it is;
His love - hers forever!
Forever, hers his!

There will be an occasion,
Affair of the heart;
When no kind of persuasion,
Will make us both part!
Exactly when, that day will come,
No person now can say;
But just for the moment,
We'll think of that day!

And as time goes by,
We'll get along fine;
Just remember I'm yours,
I'll remember you're mine!

R Bissett

WHEN LOVE WAS NEW
(To be sung to the tune of the song 'As Time Goes By')

Oh how we reminisce
And live again the bliss
Those days of me and you
When love was new
We quarrelled now and then
But we made up again
Just like most lovers do
When love was new

Chorus

When we were parted
Nothing seemed the same
So broken-hearted
Love's a cruel game
You were the one
To build my dreams upon
And make them all come true

Our course through life is set now
We never will forget how
We shared those heady days
And cherish every moment spent
When love was new

Patricia Whittle

RSVP

If Byron saw you might he write
'You walk in beauty like the night'?
Would Rabbie Burns for you compose
'My love is like a red, red rose'?
And would the Bard, as was his way,
'Compare thee to a summer's day'?

If I could like such poets be,
I'd tell you what you mean to me,
Instead I'll pen this simple line
I love you - be my Valentine!

Peter Davies

To My Valentine

Where does love come from
    Why do hearts entwine
I asked my love
    Will she forever be mine
My heart is in love
    For love cannot lie
If we were to part
    For sure I would die
My love flies so high
    As the birds in the skies
I see the love
    In the sparkle of her eyes
My love is my world
    The whole of my life
That's why in 1985
    I made Melanie my wife
I pray to the heavens
    That we never ever part
Poetry like our love
    Comes straight from the heart
I hope my love
    Will forever be mine
I pray to my love
    Please be my Valentine

Carl Fricker

CUPID'S BOW

Venus, the goddess of true love,
Sent a message from up above,
Seeing deep into my soul,
To find the one who makes me whole,

An arrow shot into my heart,
From Cupid's bow, a love-filled dart,
I opened my eyes and you were there,
My words were lost, I could only stare,

I fell in love when first I saw,
A beauty true, walk in the door,
With a single smile I melted inside,
My heart just stopped, I nearly died,

I caught my breath and then I knew,
I had fallen so deeply in love with you,
A time will come when we must part,
But always the arrow stays in my heart,

Never will I pull it out,
My love won't leave, I have no doubt,
For the arrow pierced into my soul,
And thanks to you my world is whole.

Mitch Cokien

HEAVEN AND HELL

When you make love to me I'm in Heaven,
And when you're not here I'm in Hell,
Your love is worth so much more to me,
Than anything I've got to sell:
There's no way that I could forget you,
There's more to you than I can tell,
Heavenly is the touch of your fingers,
And the brush of your sweet lips as well:
Until there's no breath in my body,
I'll sing out my love like a bell,
Sweet angel I'll love you forever,
And then a bit longer as well.

Mick Nash

MY LOVE; MY VALENTINE

Darling, be my Valentine.
My love, my Valentine forever.

Not just on this day; but every day,
Be my Valentine.

For better or worse, in sickness and in health,
Be my Valentine.

Not only this year, but in the years to come,
Darling be my Valentine.

Janet Cavill

WHAT IS LOVE
(Dedicated to my wife Miriam and 49 years of marriage)

What is love when two beings meet?
When mutual attraction is so complete?
Is it guidance of face, or some hidden force
Which unites them on their collision course?

With contradiction of magnetism and radiance,
The depth of feeling is conveyed in a glance.
Through windows of the soul the eyes reveal,
The mutual understanding of just how they feel.

No words are needed when they're meeting,
A magic silent aura completes their greeting.
Is love the perfect peace of one's inner sense,
Which accepts one another without pretence?

John Mitchell

JUST FOR YOU

Desire will kindle the passion that again
Whispers of love throughout the yearning night,
And shall I fold you in my arms until
The universe yet moves in wonder bright?

What say we bide here all the livelong day
Ne'er part again in this enchanted hour,
And time itself will gently steal away
Till all the world entire seems in flower.

Then shall we with the angels dwell
So sweet shall pass this moment's magic song
That Heaven touches us and wonderful
Is knowing that forever we belong.

Yes I shall hear your voice, my very own
And we will dwell for always close at hand
With adoration fill each fleeting year
Together voyaging a wondrous land.

Yes I have promises to keep,
And you may join me in a pledge forever -
Thus may we rare Nirvana find
Whilst parting never, never, never.

Sarah Blackmore

VALENTINE'S DAY

It's Valentine's day
but there's nothing to say
I love you more each coming day

'Tis sad to say
on Valentine's day
that love's gone cold on me today

Love and sympathy
no longer cares
it's hard to find a heart that dares

But come to spring
my heart will sing
to see the birds upon the wing

The gardens all
will bloom again
then my heart will say love's here to stay

Beth Spinks

THE SOURCE OF LOVE

In the recesses of my mind are images
struggling to maintain their messages
for the substance of your life is elusive,
quick as silver to remain exclusive.
The memories of you, held in awe,
are beliefs treasured as never before.
The trust of your being to share
stirs each dawn of day in prayer.
Words formed by my lips are sincere
though others may poison your ear.
The hope for our love is revival
resting on truth for its survival.
    My eyes are closed in concentration:
    my esteem remains without reservation.

Michael Fenton

ONE TASTE

There I stood waiting for her to appear
it had been exactly one year.
I had asked her if she would be mine
then the rose and thorn could entwine.
She had said that it would be so
but on the ground there still is snow.
Twelve months is a long time to wait
and I think it may be too late.
In the time we've been apart
someone else may have won her heart.
Here she comes to tell me she's sorry
but she no longer wants to be with me.
She has met another fella
I loved her so much but didn't tell her.
When love comes, grab it with both hands
or it will fall where it stands.
In life there is no time to waste
of true love you only get one taste.

S Glover

SO ALONE MY BOON

So alone my boon, so alone my boon
Please vow to be home soon,
For endless days I have sat wasting space
And endless nights I laid crying,
Waiting for you to fill this place.
Waiting for a warm kiss goodnight
And a heated hug when midnight strikes.

So alone my boon, so alone my boon
I wish to be a bird and fly you home so soon,
Lay you down and read you this
And tell you how much I dearly miss,
Each romantic dinner we shared
And every conversation we deeply cared,
Of our needy things that we dared to tell,
How I miss you now, I hope you're well.

So alone my boon, so alone my boon
Mornings are dragging up till noon,
Then afternoon does do the same
As I wait for you in sorrowful bane.
The task of self-pleasure is in my book
Ever since the distance you took.
Never leave me again my boon,
I wait for your return and wish it soon.

Alexander E Clarke

YOU TURNED YOUR BACK ON ME

You turned your back on me again,
It was the seventh time,
Why did you think and say with pain,
Our love wasn't worth a dime?

You left me desolate and quite alone,
For someone you thought better,
I didn't think when you didn't phone,
I would end up in the gutter.

I started drinking every day,
It was to drown my sorrow,
And when my money all was spent,
From friends I had to borrow.

I staggered lonely through the streets,
With not a place to sleep,
Pursued by policemen on their beats,
Trying the law to keep.

I went before the judge next day,
Who said, 'You'll pay some money.'
'Alas,' I said in a mannered way,
'I cannot - I have not any.'

Now I'm going to county jail,
With nothing else to see,
And all because in summer's veil,
You turned your back on me.

Joe Loxton

REMEMBERING HIM WELL

We met at a swimming pool, one morning
When our eyes first met it was so exciting
He asked me to meet him outside the swimming pool
How my heart was beating, he was so upright and tall

Remembering my very first love
'Twas like two little white doves
As they took flight on their clapped wings
Gliding with tails fanned, as their courting begins

He would take his leave from the Barracks' square
Looking forward to Friday nights, when he stood there
Opened the door, to give him a very warm welcome
As we sat there talking we felt really at home

Springtime, we would stroll around the nearby park
Listening to the melodious song, of the lark
To listen to a band playing on a fine day
As the whispering trees' leaves, began to sway

Such golden times we knew, especially under the moonlight
The guardsman to be proud of, so tall and upright
We would cuddle each other, by the fireside glow
When winter drew in, and the lights were low

After two years of courting, we did depart
Just through my obstinate, foolish heart
He came back again throughout our late teenage years
But foolishly I let him slip through my fingers

Out of his arms, and into my dreams, I dream
With memories I knew, to the lilt of a theme
His form will be with me, as if was yesterday
Just like those two doves gliding, when they flew away

Jean P McGovern

MY LOVE IS LIKE

My love is like an opening curtain
drawing back the veil of night
displaying a summer sky suffused
with rose and gold so bright

Like the early morning sunrise
that heralds a new day
and you the fragrant flower
to be opened by its sunray

My love is like a perfumed rose
that buds in late June
and you the soft summer rain
that makes it burst into bloom

My love is like a tidal wave
upon the ocean blue
that sweeps across the sea to say
I can't stop loving you

Like the fleeting hues of a rainbow
that delights you in the rain
that fills up your senses
and takes away your pain

My love is like the new moon
illuminating land and trees
like the welcome coastal lighthouse
a beacon in stormy seas

My love isn't superficial
my love is really real
and that is why I'm writing this
to tell you how I feel

Joan Magennis

COVER

Here I am, in your sweet arms
But thinking of another
A different time, a different place
A very different lover

A love that helped me stay alive
A love that wouldn't leave, or die
A love that left me feeling whole
But still a part of something more

Obsession seemed impending
But remained a distant threat
Possession, a potential thief
Of freedom, beckoned, yet

Mere happiness prevailed, and I
Habituated feeling high
But locked inside this loving space
I started looking for the door

I could have stayed cocooned by sky
Instead, I ran for cover
So, here I am, in your sweet arms
But thinking of another.

Gayna Perry

SLEEPING BEAUTY

I woke this morning to see you sleeping,
You looked so peaceful, I think you've been weeping.
I moved closer and gave you a kiss,
You smiled and awoke, it's you I miss.
We hugged and kissed, I'll miss you today,
I have to go to work like every other day.
Tonight I'm off out, I'll be all alone,
Before I go out, please telephone.
All day long, I'm thinking of you,
I've known you years, a few more than two.
Waiting for you to be my Valentine,
Can you promise to be just mine?
We can spend some time together,
I'm here for you no matter the weather.
Sweet and pure, in me you can trust,
We'll polish our love till there's no rust.
You're more precious than a single red rose,
I really like your cute little nose.
Stay with me now, you make me smile,
I've not felt so good in such a while.
Go back to sleep now and keep me warm,
Hug me real close, when there's a big storm.

Dan Del'Ouest

HONESTY

Trust in me, there are no lies,
Breathe honesty, without disguise,
You can see the truth behind the eyes,
That stare intently back.

I was the one to look at you,
And catch your eye as something new,
I don't know what it is I do?
As you stare intently back.

Holding thoughts inside my head.
Things you've done, things you've said,
These smiling eyes are easily read,
As I stare intently back.

Anna B

LOVE

Love, a word that means so much
It is a feeling you can never touch.

Love, a word that gives you strength
This lovely feeling has no length.

Love, a word with so much power
It makes you feel taller than the tallest tower.

Love, as soft as a silky sheet
Laid on a bed, nice and neat.

Love, is something we cannot resist
For without *love* we may not exist.

Richard Freeman (10)

BROADWAY IN THE RAIN

Forgotten words, nostalgic tunes,
They seem to fill my wasteland head,
A neon sign, a flash of light,
A life I sometimes leave for dead,
Reminding me of wondrous senses,
A vision honed that will remain,
And I hear heady warm cadences,
On that Broadway in the rain.

A fleeting breath, a passing sigh,
Deposits secrets in my mind,
A scarlet dress, a lipstick trace,
A passion raw and unrefined,
Excites me with a wild emotion,
Decrees a seething water main,
Erupt and make a midnight ocean,
On that Broadway in the rain.

A sweet refrain, your siren song,
Magnetically pulls me to the night;
My sheltered heart, umbrella soul,
A secret gift of second sight,
Predicting I will someday meet you,
An angel for my devil's pain,
And with a kiss I'd gently greet you,
On that Broadway in the rain.

Tony Bush

ODE TO A GIRL

Lips of crimson, an afternoon sky,
Smiling there, she made me die.
Eyes of green, an emerald sea,
Hair of rivers, so great they be.
An arrow spent, so straight and true,
Making me in love with you.
My card is played in fateful sin,
The queen of hearts, she'll always win.

O my lady, so fair and sweet,
Will our paths ever meet?
If we could join in some lost time,
The world is stopped, like in a mime.
A fiend that be in my place,
Devil's grin, angel's face.
Words have failed, not what I mean,
To this beauty I have seen.

Her heart is made of pure gold,
Love like currency, bought and sold.
See your face, throat of frog,
Eyes unclear in this thick fog.
Heart in mouth, mouth in silence,
My conscience wrestles, ends in violence.
Ice in veins, veins pump blood,
Your sweet face doth cause this flood.

My arms are short, I cannot reach,
Give me love, I do beseech.
A girl like you, there's only one,
In my solar system, my only sun.
We could be heroes, Helen of Troy,
King Agamemnon, a reckless boy.
Ancient champs in love and glory,
Some playwright to tell our story.

Hands so hot they melt a fjord,
Lips of love to fix my sword.
The sword's my heart, my heart's been broke,
A great fire that needs a stoke.
You're my flame that burns so bright,
Illuminating the darkest night.

Jason Foster

LOVE IS . . .

An understanding between two
A partnership of just me and you
To turn to when times are hard
For support, going that extra yard

Never-ending patience
Full of maintenance
Generosity and caring
Our world is about sharing

Days and nights go past
It may only be me and you that last
As the years flow
We are the ones that glow

Affection at every opportunity
I know this is meant to be
The fiery passion
We will never ration

You are my laughs
We do nothing by halves
You are my friend
Without you I could not bend

Communication never failing
To keep us plain sailing
The strength that we hold
Tight in our soul

We will always be me and you
Forever together, just us two
The warm feeling that you are near
I will no longer fear . . .

Vik

THE BOSS

My heart it beats oh so fast
Whenever you walk on past
There is a twinkle in my eye
When you come near and brush by
Is this love or infatuation
I cannot give an explanation
I know my pulse begins to zoom
When I see you enter the room
You speak to me, I start to blush
My head spins round in a rush
My stomach feels all a flutter
I can't speak, I start to stutter
You're my boss, you've no idea
I just work for you here
So each day I carry on
Trying not to be too long
Lingering over you
'Cause I've got a job to do

Tina Davis

DEAR JANE

Her name
is written in the sky after a rain.
And it's Jane.
The same
name is sweeter than wine, than sugarcane.
You know that it's Jane.

I hear
it when I'm waking or lying in bed.
Always the same.
I fear
that from that moment I'll always feel bad.
Guess that lovely name.

Dear Jane,
how could you cause me so much pain,
saying that forever you'll be here?
Cold silver's flowing through your veins,
no one to wipe my frozen tear.

Dear Jane,
how could you cause me so much pain,
saying that we will never part?
Cold silver's flowing through your veins,
frozen diamonds shimmer in your heart.

This is not what I wanted to get,
but now I just want to forget.
But, you know, it is hard
to forget the sun rose,
once you see it.
I tear this losing card,
I know, no doubt, no rose
will grow from this seed
and it's okay so . . .

Ivan Danis

LOVE IS . . .

Love is blind, not always seen,
In real life, nor in a dream.
Open your eyes, take a look around,
You might find the one to sweep you off the ground.

Love is silent, not always heard,
Loud as a drum, or as quiet as a bird.
Listen to that someone calling out your name,
When you hear that voice, you might just feel the same.

Love is words, not always said,
In a candlelit restaurant, or lying in bed.
Say what you feel or forever hold your peace,
Choose the latter and your love will cease.

Karla Bissette

UNFORGOTTEN

Although now you are far away,
long gone from my sight,
the visions of you in my mind
are still burning bright.

The clarity of my memories
will always last,
recalling those early years
and not so distant past.

Yes, these are my keepsakes,
of a much cherished era,
you'll never fade away,
your voice couldn't be clearer.

Whispers from your heart,
will eternally be heard,
those moments of connection,
without saying a word.

Wherever you may be now,
you have no need to fear,
you'll always be right by my side,
year after year.

D Cheneler

COURTING DAYS

Lovely summer days,
sweet blossom walks.
Skylarks singing,
light-hearted talks.
Shy, blushing glances,
hearts skipping a beat.
Eyes brightly shining,
with tenderness sweet.
Roving, rippling rivers,
clear, sparkling stream.
Country cottage garden,
strawberries and cream.
Picnic baskets for two,
cool green grassy glade.
Fragrance and happiness,
under cherry blossom shade.
His arm gently around me,
heavenly clouds up above.
Our happy courting days,
when we both fell in love.

Joyce Dawn Willis

EDDIE

Now then sweetie pie, what can I say?
The love for you grows more sweetly every day
Kisses tingle to the depth of my heart
Nothing compares to tear us apart
Help me not, what can I do?
I've fallen madly in love with you
The rings on our fingers makes us as one
A love binds us together, keeping us strong
Words said, there's nothing I can hide
Love is felt, indescribable inside
A wild sensation every time you're near
Sadness isn't considered, it's a happy tear
What else can I say, your love is kind
It constantly occupies my mind
Nothing in this heart is to deny
You know I love you Eddie . . . my sweetie pie.

Janine Williams